Want the facts?

Want them first?

BUY THE BOOK!

Then YOU can be the grossest person on your block, as you tell your family and friends about:

- the hairiest tongue ever found in a human mouth
- the all-time #1 collection of surgical stitches
- the most expensive booger ever sold at auction
- the only ear-wax sculpture ever made
- the longest uninterrupted (group) burping noise ever heard on the face of the earth!

If you can't be the life of the party, here's your chance to be the death of the party! (Why should you be the only one having a crummy time?!)

Books by Mel Cebulash

The Grossest Book of World Records #1
The Grossest Book of World Records #2

Published by POCKET BOOKS

THE GROSSEST

BOOK OF WORLD RECORDS #2

By
Mel Cebulash

Illustrated by Darryle Purcell

A KANGAROO BOOK
PUBLISHED BY POCKET BOOKS NEW YORK

POCKET BOOKS, a Simon & Schuster division of
GULF & WESTERN CORPORATION
1230 Avenue of the Americas, New York, N.Y. 10020

ISBN: 0-671-81175-4

First Pocket Books printing September, 1978

1 2 9 8

Trademarks registered in the United States and other countries.

Illustrated by Darryle Purcell

Printed in the U.S.A.

For
My Brother Ira

THE
GROSSEST
BOOK
OF
WORLD
RECORDS
#2

ADULT BODY
(BALDEST)

BEN SMITH OF LEXINGTON, KENTUCKY, HOLDS THE RECORD. AFTER ONE MONTH (SEPTEMBER, 1976), OUR INVESTIGATORS FOUND ONLY **TWO HAIRS** (RIGHT NOSTRIL) GROWING ON BEN'S ENTIRE BODY. "I'VE BEEN BALD SINCE BIRTH," BEN TOLD US. "ACTUALLY, I DID HAVE ANOTHER HAIR GROWING OUT OF MY LEFT NOSTRIL A FEW YEARS BACK, BUT I THINK IT DIED."

APPENDIX TRANSPLANT
⟨FROM HOG⟩

JOSEF PODLAWSKI, OF WARSAW, POLAND, HOLDS THE RECORD. ON JANUARY 14, 1971, DOCTORS REMOVED JOSEF'S APPENDIX AND REPLACED IT WITH A HOG'S APPENDIX. AS OF JANUARY 14, 1977 (6 YEARS LATER), JOSEF'S TRANSPLANTED APPENDIX WAS FUNCTIONING WELL, AND DOCTORS FOLLOWING HIS PROGRESS EXPRESSED NO CONCERN ABOUT HIS DESIRE TO EAT MEALS OUT OF A SLOP BUCKET.

ARMPIT
(SNIFFING)

MIRIAM MORTON, OF SOW'S BOTTOM, MINNESOTA, HOLDS THE RECORD. THROUGH SEPTEMBER 8, 1978, MIRIAM HAS SNIFFED THE ARMPITS OF 42,375 PEOPLE. "PEOPLE LINE UP TO LET ME DO IT," MIRIAM TOLD US. "THEY'RE TICKLED AT THE OPPORTUNITY, AND BECAUSE I KEEP LISTS OF THEIR NAMES, THEY KNOW THEY HAVE A SHARE IN THE RECORD."

BEEF HEARTS

(COLLECTION)

HANS KROGER, A RETIRED BUTCHER IN MUNICH, GERMANY, HAS THE WORLD'S LARGEST COLLECTION OF BEEF HEARTS. AS OF MAY 14, 1978, HANS HAD OVER **700** HEARTS IN HIS COLLECTION. HE KEEPS THEM IN A HUGE FREEZER. "ONCE A MONTH, I TAKE THEM OUT AND INSPECT THEM," HANS TOLD OUR INVESTIGATOR. "SOME ARE VERY OLD, BUT THEY'RE VERY FINE. I SUPPOSE THEY'LL BE EATEN AFTER I DIE. I HAVE NO CHILDREN TO CARE FOR THEM."

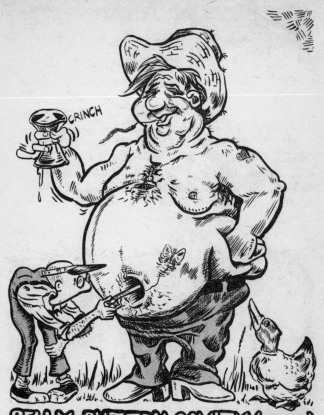

CRINCH

BELLY BUTTON CAVITY (DEPTH)

GEORGE YOUNG, OF FAT GUT, OKLAHOMA, HOLDS THE RECORD. IN A TEST HELD ON MARCH 27, 1974, AN UNSHARPENED PENCIL WAS INSERTED INTO GEORGE'S BELLY BUTTON CAVITY. THE PENCIL REACHED A DEPTH OF **7 INCHES** BEFORE IT TOUCHED GEORGE'S BELLY BUTTON. (**NOTE**: WHEN THE PENCIL WAS WITHDRAWN, IT WAS NOT, AS SOME NEWSPAPERS HAVE REPORTED, SHARPENED.)

13

BELLY-BUTTON LINT (FROM THE STARS)

BARRY BARBER OF LOS ANGELES, HOLDS THE RECORD. BARRY HAS OVER **14 POUNDS** (1978) OF BELLY-BUTTON LINT VACUUMED FROM THE STARS. "I USE A HAND-VAC," BARRY TOLD US. "THE STARS DON'T LIKE TO BE TOUCHED, BUT ASIDE FROM THAT, THEY'RE DARN DECENT PEOPLE. ONE REALLY BIG STAR, AND I'M NOT GOING TO NAME HIM, GIVES ME ABOUT AN OUNCE OF LINT A MONTH FOR NOTHING, AND HE COULD SELL IT, BELIEVE ME."

BOOGERS (FROM HISTORY)

DR. HANS FRIEDLINK,
OF CAMBRIDGE, MASSACHUSETTS,
HAS BEEN COLLECTING BOOGERS
FROM HISTORICAL FIGURES FOR OVER 30
YEARS. HIS COLLECTION NUMBERS **148**
AND COMES FROM THE NOSES OF THE
MOST IMPORTANT FIGURES OF THE
TWENTIETH CENTURY. "I GUESS MY MOST
INTERESTING BOOGER IS A FROZEN ONE
THAT FELL FROM THE NOSE OF ADMIRAL
PEARY DURING ONE OF HIS EXPEDITIONS,"
DR. FRIEDLINK TOLD US.

BOOGER
(HIGHEST PRICED)

A BOOGER AUCTIONED OFF AT A NEW YORK CITY GALLERY BROUGHT THE RECORD PRICE OF $105,000. THIS IS, AS FAR AS WE KNOW, THE RECORD PRICE PAID FOR A BOOGER. IT WAS PRESERVED PERFECTLY AND WAS REPUTED TO HAVE COME FROM THE NOSE OF **CZAR NICHOLAS** OF RUSSIA. (**NOTE:** THE IDENTITY OF THE BIDDER WAS NOT MADE PUBLIC.)

BURPING
(GROUP)

THIS RECORD BELONGS TO THE PEOPLE OF GASSUP, NEW MEXICO (POPULATION 752). IN A TAPED SESSION ON JANUARY 14, 1975, THE PEOPLE OF GASSUP RECORDED AN UN-BROKEN BURPING NOISE THAT LASTED FOR **14 HOURS AND 39 MINUTES**. (NOTE: THE TAPE WAS PLAYED INTO THE CONGRESSIONAL RECORD ON JANUARY 28, 1975.)

"GASSUP N.M. GROSSEST BOOK OR BUST"

19

CALLUS (COLLECTION)

FLORENCE FRANKLIN OF PEORIA, ILLINOIS, HOLDS THE RECORD. AS OF SEPTEMBER 12, 1978, FLORENCE HAD OVER **200 POUNDS** OF CALLUS IN HER COLLECTION. "I SHAVE IT OFF PEOPLE," FLORENCE TOLD US. "THEY DON'T MIND. SOME PEOPLE EVEN AUTOGRAPH THE BIG PIECES."

CAT BITES

MAURICE MORRIS, OF NINE LIVES, KENTUCKY, HOLDS THE RECORD. THROUGH 1977, MAURICE HAD BEEN THE VICTIM OF **1,649** CAT BITES. "I'M PROUD OF THIS RECORD BECAUSE I REALLY HAD TO WORK FOR IT," MAURICE TOLD US. "CATS PREFER TO SCRATCH."

CAT TEETH
(COLLECTION)

MARGIE NORMAN, OF NEWARK, NEW JERSEY HOLDS THE RECORD. THROUGH 1976, MARGIE'S COLLECTION OF CAT TEETH NUMBERED **5,139**. "I USED TO BUY THEM," MARGIE TOLD US, "BUT LATELY MANY WONDERFUL PEOPLE HAVE BEEN SENDING THEM TO ME. THEY KNOW I'LL TAKE GOOD CARE OF THE TEETH. I LOVE EVERY TOOTH IN MY COLLECTION."

CATERPILLAR EATING (LIVE)

WALTER LUCAS OF DENVER HOLDS THE RECORD. IN A CONTEST HELD ON LABOR DAY, 1974, WALTER ATE 17 LIVE CATERPILLARS IN **22** MINUTES. THE 17TH, A GREEN ONE, BROKE A TIE AND GAVE WALTER THE RECORD. "MY PLAN WAS TO SWALLOW THEM WHOLE," WALTER TOLD US, "BUT I HAD A SORE THROAT. SO I CHEWED THEM. I WAS REAL PLEASED THAT I COULD DO IT." SO ARE WE, WALTER!

CB RADIO
(GROSSEST HANDLE)

AS FAR AS WE CAN TELL, **JESSE WALLACE** OF MOBILE, ALABAMA, DESERVES THIS RECORD. JESSE'S HANDLE IS **BIG PUKE FROM MOBILE.** "I TRAVEL AROUND AND TALK TO A LOT OF PEOPLE," JESSE TOLD US, "BUT NO ONE EVER ANSWERS ME. I'M GETTING A BETTER SENDING UNIT, AND IF THAT DOESN'T WORK, I'M GETTING A NEW HANDLE." SOUNDS LIKE THE UNIT, JESSE, SO KEEP CALLING!

CEMETARY SLEEPING

WILMA WALTERS, OF MORBIDITY FALLS, MICHIGAN, HOLDS THE RECORD, THROUGH 1977, WILMA HAD SLEPT IN 1,495 CEMETERIES IN NORTH AMERICA AND EUROPE. "I LIKE THE PEACE AND QUIET OF A CEMETERY," WILMA TOLD US. "HOTELS AND MOTELS ARE JUST TOO NOISY."

CHICKEN BONES (COLLECTION)

IN A COOPERATIVE EFFORT, THE TOWNSPEOPLE OF CHAPMAN, NEW YORK (POP. 3,768), ATE AT THE COLONEL'S EVERY DAY FOR A YEAR (1975-76). BY SAVING THEIR BONES, THE PEOPLE ACCUMULATED **12,573 POUNDS** OF BONES. (**NOTE**: THIS IS AN APPROXIMATE WEIGHT, SINCE MANY OF THE BONES HAD MEAT ON THEM.)

CIGAR BUTTS
(COLLECTION)

LARRY LINCOLN, OF TAMPA, FLORIDA, HOLDS
THE RECORD. AS OF JANUARY 14, 1978, LARRY'S
COLLECTION OF CIGAR BUTTS NUMBERED **23,345**
LARRY, 72, HAS BEEN COLLECTING BUTTS FOR
60 YEARS. "I REFUSE DONATIONS," LARRY
TOLD US. "I'VE DEVOTED MY WHOLE LIFE TO
COLLECTING CIGAR BUTTS, AND I DON'T NEED
ANY HELP AT THIS STAGE."

CLAPPING (GROUP)

THE PEOPLE OF **BIG HAND**, VIRGINIA, HOLD THE RECORD. AS OF APRIL, 1977, THERE HAS BEEN A RESIDENT OF BIG HAND CLAPPING IN THE TOWN'S SQUARE EVERY MINUTE OF EVERY HOUR OF EVERY DAY SINCE APRIL, 1927 (**50 YEARS**). "WE WELCOME NEWCOMERS," THE MAYOR OF BIG HAND TOLD US, "BUT THOSE WHO DON'T WANT TO SHARE IN THE CLAPPING SHOULD MOVE ELSEWHERE. WE BELIEVE IN WORKING TOGETHER." AND ANYONE WHO MOVES THERE DESERVES A BIG HAND!

SLURP

COBWEB (EATING)

ROBERT ARMSTRONG OF GREENWICH, CONNECTICUT, HOLDS THE RECORD. IN A CONTEST HELD ON MAY 3, 1973, ROBERT ATE **742** COBWEBS IN LESS THAN FIVE MINUTES. "I TRAINED FOR THE RECORD," ROBERT TOLD US, "BUT I NEVER WOULD HAVE GUESSED I COULD EAT THAT MANY COBWEBS. THEY TASTE BETTER THAN MOST PEOPLE THINK."

DANDRUFF
(EATING)

FOR CENTURIES, THE PEOPLE OF **GOTSHAIR**, A
SMALL ISLAND IN THE ATLANTIC, HAVE THRIVED
ON A DIET (PARTIAL) OF DANDRUFF. THEY HAVE
THE RECORD BECAUSE THEY ARE THE ONLY OPEN
DANDRUFF EATERS. (REPORTS OF CLOSET DAN-
DRUFF EATERS HAVE NEVER BEEN SUBSTANTIATED.)
IN 1974 A DANDRUFF DROUGHT THREATENED THE
HEALTH OF THE PEOPLE OF **GOTSHAIR**, BUT DO-
NATIONS FROM THE PEOPLE OF TEGRIN, NEW
JERSEY, EASED THE PROBLEM UNTIL THE
DROUGHT ENDED.

DEAD ANIMAL IDENTIFICATION
⟨BY SNIFFING⟩

DR. HANS KLEIBER OF VIENNA IS THE WORLD'S GREATEST DEAD ANIMAL IDENTIFIER. IN A TEST ON AUGUST 12, 1975, DR. KLEIBER SUCCESSFULLY IDENTIFIED **43** DEAD ANIMALS BY SNIFFING AT THEIR REMAINS. OF COURSE, DR. KLEIBER WAS BLINDFOLDED DURING THE TEST. "TO BE HONEST," DR. KLEIBER HUMBLY ADMITTED, "I ALMOST MISSED ON THE MUSKRAT. IT SMELLED LIKE A HORSE."

DEAD BATS
⟨COLLECTION⟩

DAN BLAKE, OF BLOODSTONE, NEW YORK, HOLDS THE RECORD. DAN HAD **298** DEAD BATS IN THE BACK OF HIS DRUGSTORE IN 1976. "I'D RATHER HAVE LIVE BATS," DAN TOLD US, "BUT MY CUSTOMERS ARE STRANGE. THEY OBJECT TO LIVE BATS."

DEAD INSECT (COLLECTION)

PAUL ROACH, OF LADY PORT, NEW HAMPSHIRE, HOLDS THE RECORD. DURING 1977, PAUL'S DEAD INSECT COLLECTION WENT OVER THE **ONE MILLION** MARK. "THAT'S IT FOR ME," PAUL ANNOUNCED. "I'VE HAD IT WITH DEAD INSECTS." (**NOTE**: AN UNCONFIRMED REPORT INDICATES THAT PAUL HAS CHANGED HIS MIND AND IS COLLECTING AGAIN.)

DIET (HEALTHIEST)

RESIDENTS OF THE SMALL TOWN OF **NATURE'S BEST**, CALIFORNIA, SEEM TO HAVE THE WORLD'S HEALTH-IEST DIET. IT CONSISTS OF A DAILY SPOONFUL OF ORGANIC HAIR LICE. (**NOTE:** THE AVERAGE AGE IN NATURE'S BEST IS 97, AND THE OLDEST RES-IDENT IS 193.) "WE WANT NEWCOMERS," THE MAYOR OF NATURE'S BEST TOLD US, "BUT WE DIS-COURAGE BALD PEOPLE. WE WANT PEOPLE WHO ARE ABLE TO FEED THEMSELVES."

EAR WAX
(SCULPTURE)

GLENDA RAMBEAU'S, "THE HORSE," A 14-INCH SCULPTURE, IS MADE ENTIRELY OF EAR WAX, AND IS, ACCORDING TO OUR RECORDS, THE ONLY EAR WAX SCULPTURE EVER MADE. GLENDA UNVEILED THE SCULPTURE AT A SHOW IN PARIS IN 1974. "I LIKE WORKING IN EAR WAX," GLENDA TOLD EXCITED SPECTATORS. "IT MAKES YOU FEEL AS IF YOU'RE PART OF THE WORK."

EAR WAX LICKING (FROM PAY TELEPHONES)

DAN DANNON OF NEW YORK CITY HOLDS THE RECORD. BY HIS OWN COUNT (UNOFFICIAL), DAN HAS LICKED EAR WAX FROM THE RECEIVERS OF MORE THAN **ONE MILLION** PAY PHONES. BY OUR COUNT, DAN LICKED 43,579 RECEIVERS DURING 1975, AND THIS, OF COURSE, WAS SUFFICIENT FOR THE RECORD. TELEPHONE COMPANY OFFICIALS ARE DISTURBED BY DAN'S ACTIONS AND HAVE APPEALED TO FEDERAL AUTHORITIES TO RULE AGAINST RECEIVER LICKING.

EYE GOOK
(COLLECTION)

SANDMAN PHILLIPS, OF BOSTON, HOLDS THE
RECORD. AS OF MAY 2, 1977, SANDMAN HAD
47,398 SEPARATE PIECES OF EYE GOOK IN
HIS COLLECTION WHICH COMES FROM
PEOPLE ALL OVER THE WORLD. "I AM NOW
COLLECTING EYE GOOK FROM ANIMALS,"
SANDMAN INFORMED US. "I GOT INTERESTED
AFTER A FRIEND IN SAUDI ARABIA SENT ME
SOME CAMEL EYE GOOK. IT WAS REALLY GROSS."

EYE GOOK
(EATING)

MIMI MURINE, 103, OF BARCELONA, SPAIN, HOLDS THE RECORD. EACH MORNING SINCE SHE WAS TEN (**NOTE:** VERIFIED BY LIE DETECTOR TEST), MIMI HAS STARTED HER DAY BY EATING HER EYE GOOK. "I DON'T KNOW IF EYE GOOK HAS HAD ANYTHING TO DO WITH MY LONG LIFE," MIMI TOLD US IN 1977, "BUT I DO KNOW THAT I LOVE THE TASTE OF IT."

FEET
(HAIRIEST)

GEORGE BOYD, OF MONTROSE, CALIFORNIA, HOLDS THE RECORD. GEORGE'S FEET ARE FULLY COVERED WITH HAIR (BROWN) AND HAVE BEEN SINCE HIS BIRTH IN 1930. "I USED TO SHAVE THEM," GEORGE TOLD US, "BUT I GOT TIRED OF STARING AT MY FEET IN THE MIRROR EVERY MORNING. THE ONLY THING I HATE TO DO IS GO SWIMMING IN A POOL. THE LIFEGUARDS ALWAYS TELL ME TO TAKE MY SOCKS OFF."

FEET (SMELL)

ON AUGUST 21, 1976, **WANDA LAKE**, 18, BROKE THE
RECORD HELD BY GEORGE DAVID. WANDA RE-
MOVED HER SHOES IN THE CROWDED LOBBY OF
A LOS ANGELES THEATER. IN THE FIVE MIN-
UTES THAT FOLLOWED, THE LOBBY WAS A
CHAOTIC MASS OF PANIC-STRICKEN PEOPLE
TRYING DESPERATELY TO ESCAPE. IN THE
END, 42 PEOPLE WERE SICK, AND 14 OTHERS
HAD PASSED OUT.

FILLINGS ⟨FROM TEETH⟩

BRIAN GAPSMORE, OF HEREFORD, ENGLAND, HOLDS THE RECORD. AS OF 1975, BRIAN'S COLLECTION OF TOOTH FILLINGS WEIGHED OVER **ONE TON**. "PEOPLE SEND ME TEETH THAT HAVE BEEN PULLED, AND I REMOVE THE FILLINGS," BRIAN TOLD US. "IT'S A VERY PLEASANT WAY TO PASS THE TIME, TINKERING WITH TEETH FROM ALL OVER THE WORLD."

FISH EYE
(EATING)

IKO YAMAGROSSO, OF TOKYO, JAPAN, HOLDS THE RECORD. IN A CONTEST HELD ON MARCH 23, 1974, IKO ATE **4,321** RAW FISH EYES IN LESS THAN AN HOUR. HIS CLOSEST COMPETITOR, SEAN O'SHEA OF DUBLIN, IRELAND, PASSED OUT AFTER CONSUMING 3,932 EYES. "I SWALLOWED THEM WHOLE," IKO EXPLAINED TO US. "SEAN CHEWED THEM. THAT'S WHY HE GOT TIRED."

FISH HEAD (COLLECTION)

JANICE KARP OF WEHAWKEN, NEW JERSEY, HOLDS THE RECORD. AS OF SEPTEMBER 12, 1976, JANICE HAD **3,459** FISH HEADS IN HER COLLECTION. "MY RECORD WILL BE TOPPED," JANICE TOLD US, "I CAN'T COLLECT ANY MORE HEADS. THE SMELL IS GETTING TO ME. I NEVER THOUGHT IT WOULD, BUT IT IS."

FROG SKIN
(COLLECTION)

BARBARA NEWSOME, OF BLUFFTON, INDIANA HOLDS THE RECORD. ON MARCH 12, 1973, BARBARA'S COLLECTION OF FROG SKINS NUMBERED 31,742. "I USED TO CATCH THE FROGS MYSELF," BARBARA TOLD US, "BUT NOW I JUST PAY KIDS A NICKEL A SKIN, AND IT GIVES THEM SOMETHING WORTHWHILE TO DO DURING THE SUMMER."

GARBAGE OF THE STARS

JACK KENO, OF LOS ANGELES, HOLDS THE RECORD. EACH DAY SANITATION WORKERS FROM NEARBY BEVERLY HILLS DELIVER GARBAGE COLLECTED FROM MOVIE STARS' HOMES TO JACK'S STORE—THE GAG BAG. "I SELL IT UNOPENED," JACK TOLD US. "YOU'D BE SURPRISED AT HOW MANY PEOPLE WANT GARBAGE FROM THE STARS." JACK USUALLY HAS A TON IN STOCK, AND HE'S ALSO INVESTIGATING WAYS TO SELL GARBAGE THRU THE MAIL.

GARLIC
⟨EATING⟩

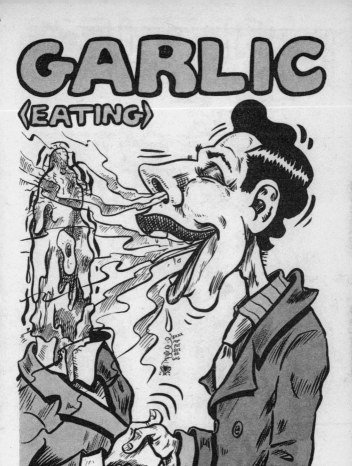

JOSEPH VAN DYKE OF PRINCETON, NEW JERSEY, HOLDS THE RECORD. ON JANUARY 14, 1976, JOSEPH CONSUMED **197** CLOVES OF GARLIC IN 42 MINUTES. AFTER THIS EXHIBITION, JOSEPH ATTEMPTED TO THANK PEOPLE WHO HAD APPLAUDED HIS RECORD-BREAKING FEAT, AND SEVERAL OF THEM WERE INJURED IN THE SUBSEQUENT STAMPEDE.

HAIRIEST LEGS
⟨ADULT⟩

RITA SIMS OF EL PASO, TEXAS HOLDS THIS RECORD. RITA'S LEGS ARE ENTIRELY COVERED WITH HAIR (**NOTE**: CHECKED IN 1975.) OTHERS HAVE THE SAME AMOUNT OF HAIR ON THEIR THIGHS AND CALVES, BUT RITA'S FEET, INCLUDING THE BOTTOMS, ARE ALSO COVERED WITH HAIR. "I TRY TO KEEP OFF MY FEET," RITA TOLD US. "I'D HATE TO WEAR THE HAIR OFF AND LOSE THE RECORD."

HAIRIEST LEGS
(CHILD)

THIS RECORD BELONGS TO FRANK ALBERTO OF
CULVER, COLORADO. AT AGE TWO (1976), FRANK'S
LEGS AND ARMS WERE ENTIRELY COVERED WITH
HAIR, EXCEPT FOR BALD PATCHES ON HIS KNEES.
"HE'S SO CUTE," FRANK'S MOTHER TOLD US. "HE
CRAWLS AROUND THE HOUSE LIKE A LITTLE TEDDY
BEAR. I IMAGINE I'LL BE A LITTLE SAD WHEN
HE STARTS WALKING." SO WILL YOUR NEIGHBORS.

HEIGHT AND WEIGHT DIVINATION (THROUGH SEAT ANALYSIS)

SUBODH REY, OF NEW DELHI, INDIA, IS THE WORLDS GREATEST SEAT ANALYZER. DURING A TELEVISED APPEARANCE IN THE U.S., SUBODH CORRECTLY GAVE THE HEIGHT AND WEIGHT OF 20 PERSONS AFTER QUICKLY SNIFFING THE CHAIRS ON WHICH THEY HAD BEEN SEATED. "I CAN'T EXPLAIN IT," SUBODH TOLD US. "IT'S A GIFT."

HUMAN LAWNMOWER

PATRICIA LINDEN, OF CHICAGO, ILLINOIS, IS THE WORLD'S GREATEST GRASS EATER. IN A TEST HELD ON JULY 4, 1976, PATRICIA CHEWED UP ALL OF THE INFIELD GRASS AT CHICAGO'S WRIGLEY FIELD. PEOPLE WATCHING THIS PRE-GAME TEST GAVE PATRICIA A STANDING OVATION. "SHE'S BETTER THAN A LAWNMOWER," ONE GROUNDSKEEPER TOLD US.

INFESTATION BY MITES (GROUP)

THIS RECORD BELONGS TO THE 3,859 RESIDENTS OF **ITCHY BUTT, MONTANA.** IN 1974, VISITING DOCTORS CERTIFIED THAT EVERY PERSON IN THE TOWN WAS SUFFERING FROM SCABIES, A SKIN DISEASE CAUSED BY MITE INFECTION. "THE MITES SEEMED TO BE JUMPING FROM ONE PERSON TO ANOTHER," THE MAYOR OF ITCHY BUTT TOLD US, "SO WE DECIDED TO GET TOGETHER AND GO FOR THE RECORD."

SMOOCH

KISS OF DOG
(LONGEST)

EVELYN HUNT OF LOS ANGELES HOLDS THE
RECORD. ON NOVEMBER 5, 1976, EVELYN
PLANTED HER LIPS ON JODIE, AN 11-YEAR-
OLD MONGREL, AND HELD THEM ON THE
DOG'S LIPS FOR **SEVEN MINUTES**. EVELYN
WAS DELIGHTED WITH HER RECORD-MAKING
KISS. HOWEVER, JODIE WASN'T AS PLEASED.
AFTER THE ORDEAL, SHE REFUSED TO EAT
AND HAD TO BE TREATED BY AN ANIMAL
PSYCHIATRIST FROM BEVERLY HILLS.

54

LEFTOVER EATING

LILLIAN BINGAM, 78, CLAIMED THE RECORD IN 1974. FOR OVER **OVER 50 YEARS** (NOTE: STILL NOT VERIFIED), LILLIAN HAS BEEN SLIPPING INTO SEATS IN CAFETERIAS AND EATING LEFTOVERS. "I WATCH OUT FOR THIN PEOPLE," LILLIAN TOLD US. "THEY NEVER FINISH THEIR DESSERT."

LEFTOVER POPCORN (COLLECTION)

FRED MORGAN, 17, OF HAMMOND, INDIANA, HOLDS THE RECORD. AS OF JULY 22, 1978, THE TWO-CAR GARAGE BEHIND FRED'S HOME WAS FILLED WITH LEFTOVER POPCORN. TO WARD OFF CHALLENGERS, FRED PLANS TO FLATTEN THE POPCORN AND GIVE HIMSELF MORE SPACE IN THE GARAGE. "I GET MOST OF IT FROM LOCAL MOVIE THEATERS," FRED TOLD US. "MOST PEOPLE DON'T FINISH THEIR POPCORN. I'D HAVE MORE IN MY COLLECTION, BUT SOMETIMES I EAT THE BUTTERED LEFTOVERS. I REALLY LIKE BUTTERED POPCORN."

LIVE SNAIL-SUCKING

ARMAND FORCALQUIER, OF MARSEILLE, FRANCE,
HOLDS THE RECORD. IN A CONTEST HELD ON
FEBRUARY 12, 1974, ARMAND SUCKED DOWN
1,238 LIVE SNAILS IN A LITTLE OVER 4 HOURS.
"IT WAS NOT EASY," ARMAND BOASTED AFTER
HE LEARNED THAT THE RECORD WAS HIS.
"THEY CLING TO THEIR SHELLS, BUT THEY
CAN'T GET AWAY FROM ME."

LONGEST BATH (GROUP)

THE RESIDENTS OF **CULLIGAN**, MONTANA, SHARE THIS RECORD. ON JUNE 14, 1974, ALL 323 OF THEM CLIMBED INTO THEIR BATHTUBS. TWO FULL WEEKS LATER, THEY CLIMBED OUT AND CLAIMED THE RECORD. "IT WASN'T EASY TO LIVE IN A BATHTUB FOR TWO WEEKS," ONE RESIDENT TOLD US, "BUT WE WANTED THE WORLD TO KNOW THAT THE PEOPLE OF **CULLIGAN** AREN'T SOFT."

MILK BONES
(EATING)

IN A CONTEST HELD ON APRIL 26, 1973, LARRY "LASSIE" LINCOLN SET THE RECORD. LARRY ATE **794** MILK BONES IN LESS THAN AN HOUR. LARRY'S CLOSEST COMPETITOR PASSED OUT AFTER EATING 511 MILK BONES AND HAD TO BE TREATED BY A VET, AS THE ATTENDING DOCTOR CLAIMED SHE DIDN'T KNOW THE ANTIDOTE FOR AN OVERDOSE OF MILK BONES.

MUSCLES
(FOREARMS)

ARNOLD WEEDNER, 22, HAS THE WORLD'S
LARGEST FOREARMS. EACH OF ARNOLDS FORE-
ARMS MEASURES **24 INCHES** FLEXED (1975).
ARNOLD, WHO WEIGHS 478 POUNDS TOLD US:
"THERE'S NOT AN OUNCE OF FAT ON MY
FOREARMS."

MUSCLES (LATS)

JOANNA SHEPHERD, 24, HAS THE WORLD'S BEST DEVELOPED LATS. "I DIDN'T REALIZE THEY WERE SO WELL-DEVELOPED," JOANNA TOLD US, "UNTIL THE DAY I DISCOVERED I COULD FLY." (NOTE: JOANNA RECENTLY STARRED IN AERO FILMS' THE BAT LADY OF PARIS.)

61

MUSCLES
(THIGH)

JUDY BURNS, 19, OF NEW YORK CITY, HAS THE WORLD'S LARGEST THIGH. JUDY'S RIGHT THIGH MEASURES **44 INCHES** FLEXED (1977), AND SHE CLAIMS IT'S A RESULT OF BIKE RIDING. "I'M A LITTLE WORRIED ABOUT MY LEFT THIGH," JUDY TOLD US. "IT HASN'T RESPONDED."

NOSE STUFFING
⟨LIMBURGER CHEESE⟩

HANS KLEIBER, OF WEST BERLIN HOLDS THE
RECORD. IN A CONTEST HELD ON MAY 1, 1974,
HANS MANAGED TO STUFF **13 OUNCES** OF LIM-
BURGER CHEESE INTO HIS NOSTRILS IN LESS
THAN A MINUTE. HANS' CLOSEST COMPETITOR
GAGGED ON NINE OUNCES AND WAS
DISQUALIFIED.

NOSTRIL HAIR
(COLLECTION)

ALICE DRISTON, OF DENVER, HOLDS THE
RECORD. AS OF 1977, ALICE'S COLLECTION
NUMBERS 11,894 SEPARATE NOSTRIL HAIRS.
"NO TWO HAIRS COME FROM THE SAME
NOSTRIL," ALICE REPORTED, "BUT I'VE
TWEEZED TWO FROM THE SAME NOSE.
PEOPLE WHO COOPERATE USUALLY DON'T
MIND GIVING TWO."

PERSPIRATION
⟨COLLECTION⟩

RESIDENTS OF SWEET SWEAT, TEXAS, CAN BE PROUD OF THEMSELVES. USING THE MOTTO "EVERY LITTLE DRIP COUNTS," THEY MANAGED TO COLLECT **42 GALLONS** OF PERSPIRATION DURING THE SUMMER OF 1975. (**NOTE:** OUNCE BOTTLES FROM THE COLLECTION CAN BE PURCHASED FROM THE SWEET SWEAT BOTTLING CO., SWEET SWEAT, TEXAS.)

PLATE LICKING

GLORIA EVANS, 62, HOLDS THE RECORD.
GLORIA CLAIMS THAT SHE HAS LICKED
OVER A MILLION PLATES IN THE FORTY
YEARS IN WHICH SHE HAS BEEN LICKING.
"IF I GET TO BE FRIENDS WITH THE KIT-
CHEN HELP IN A BIG PLACE, THEY'LL OFTEN
LET ME LICK ALL THE PLATES BEFORE THEY
WASH THEM," GLORIA TOLD US. "ON A GOOD
NIGHT, I COULD GET TO LICK ABOUT 600
PLATES. THAT'S A LOT OF LICKING." IT SURE
IS, GLORIA!

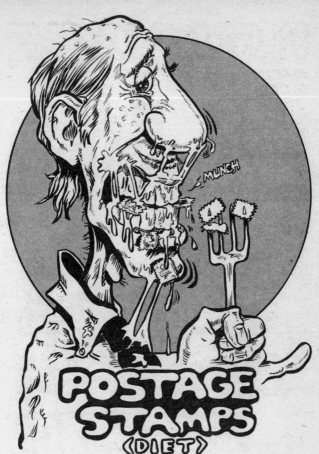

POSTAGE STAMPS
⟨DIET⟩

HERBERT WINSTEAD, A POSTAL CLERK FROM
TRUE GLUE, KENTUCKY HOLDS THE RECORD.
TO CONTROL HIS WEIGHT, HERBERT HAS BEEN
EATING POSTAGE STAMPS FOR LUNCH FOR
OVER TEN YEARS. (NOTE: HERBERT'S CO-
WORKERS VERIFIED HIS RECORD.) "BE SURE
YOU MAKE THE POINT THAT THEY'RE CAN-
CELED," HERBERT TOLD US. "I DON'T WANT TO
LOSE MY MEAL TICKET."

PULLING (WITH GUMS)

CARL HEMBUCK, 82, HOLDS THE RECORD. AT THE ANNUAL SENIOR CITIZEN'S PICNIC (JULY 4, 1977) IN COLUMBIA, SOUTH CAROLINA, CARL MANAGED TO PULL A WAGON LOADED WITH SENIOR CITIZENS (WEIGHING 3,874 POUNDS) A DISTANCE OF **500** YARDS. CARL MANAGED THIS AMAZING FEAT WITH THE WAGON HANDLE HELD BETWEEN HIS GUMS. WE, AT THE GROSSEST, SALUTE THIS WONDERFUL OLD-TIMER!

RAT TAILS COLLECTION

GLENDA GABOR OF PHILADELPHIA HOLDS THE RECORD. AS OF JUNE, 1978, GLENDA HAD **35,432** RAT TAILS IN HER COLLECTION. "I WEAVE THEM TOGETHER," GLENDA TOLD US, "AND MAKE LITTLE RUGS FOR MY APARTMENT. THEY'RE QUITE A SENSATION TO BARE FEET," AND THEY'RE NICE TO LIE ON, TOO, GLENDA!

RAW KIDNEY
(EATING)

ALICE CALDWELL OF BUTTE, MONTANA, HOLDS
THE RECORD. ON OCTOBER 22, 1975, ALICE GOBBLED
UP MORE THAN **14 POUNDS** OF RAW VEAL AND LAMB
KIDNEYS. "KIDNEYS ARE A GOOD SOURCE OF PRO-
TEINS AND VITAMINS," ALICE TOLD US. "IF YOU
COOK THEM, YOU LOSE SOME OF THE VITAMINS.
AS YOU CAN SEE, I DON'T CARE ABOUT THE
RECORD—I CARE ABOUT MY HEALTH."

70

RAW TONGUE
(EATING)

MIKE McCOY OF COWLICK, TEXAS, HOLDS THE RECORD. ON NOVEMBER 3, 1975, MIKE CONSUMED 7½ POUNDS OF RAW BEEF TONGUE IN 22 MINUTES. "I EAT IT FAST," MIKE TOLD US. "IT TASTES TERRIBLE, BUT I'D DO ANYTHING TO BE ONE OF THE GROSSEST."

ROACH (HIGHEST PRICE)

HOWARD YOUS HOLDS THE RECORD. IN AN AUCTION HELD ON MAY 6, 1975, HOWARD PAID **$112,450** FOR LASSIE II, A ONE-YEAR OLD ROACH OWNED BY SHEILA CIDERMAN OF NEW YORK. "ANYONE WHO KNOWS ANYTHING ABOUT ROACHES KNOWS THAT THIS ONE COMES FROM CHAMPION STOCK," HOWARD TOLD US. (NOTE: HOWARD DIED A FEW MONTHS AFTER THE AUCTION, AND THE COURT BATTLE FOR CUSTODY OF THE ROACH WAS STILL IN PROGRESS AT THIS WRITING.)

LASSIE II

SOLD

ROACH
(LARGEST)

RITA CARSON, OF PASADENA, CALIFORNIA, CLAIMS THE RECORD FOR HAVING RAISED THE WORLD'S LARGEST ROACH. HER RECORD-SETTING ROACH IS OVER A FOOT LONG AND WEIGHS CLOSE TO **TWO POUNDS** (1976). "PLENTY OF PROTEIN," RITA TOLD US, "AND PLENTY OF GOOD, NATURAL VITAMINS HELPED TO MAKE THIS ROACH INTO A CHAMPION. YOU SHOULD HAVE SEEN IT WHEN I FIRST FOUND IT CRAWLING AROUND MY KITCHEN."

ROACH
(LONGEST LIVING)

LASSIE, A 12-YEAR-OLD ROACH OWNED BY
SHEILA BIDERMAN (1975), IS PROBABLY THE
LONGEST LIVING ROACH IN RECORDED HIS-
TORY. "I'M HONORED TO SEE LASSIE GET IN
THE RECORD BOOK," SHEILA TOLD US. "SHE'S
ALMOST LIKE A MEMBER OF THE FAMILY,
AND IF SHE GETS TOO OLD TO POKE AROUND
THE FOOD BY HERSELF, YOU CAN BET I'LL
DO THE HUMANE THING AND STEP ON HER—
RECORD OR NO RECORD."

74

HANS GROSCHSCHMIDT, OF HAMBURG, WEST
GERMANY, HOLDS THE RECORD. ON OCTOBER
15, 1972, HANS DOWNED **33 QUARTS** OF SAUER-
KRAUT JUICE IN 45 MINUTES. ALTHOUGH
HANS WAS RETCHING IN AGONY AFTER HIS
RECORD-SETTING FEAT, HE MANAGED TO TELL
US, "I LOVE SAUERKRAUT JUICE."

SINGING GROUP (GROSSEST NAME)

THIS RECORD WAS DECIDED BY A NATIONWIDE SURVEY. OF THE 5,000 MEN, WOMEN, AND CHILDREN POLLED, 4,898 VOTED FOR THE WINNING GROUP. THE WINNING GROUP IS **BOOGERS ON TOAST.** "WE APPRECIATE THE PLUG, MAN," THE GROUP'S LEADER TOLD US, "BUT WE DON'T REGARD THE NAME AS GROSS."

SNAIL SUCKING
⟨DEAD⟩

PIERRE LA TOCHE OF PARIS HOLDS THE RECORD. IN A CONTEST HELD ON DECEMBER 12, 1974, PIERRE SUCKED **243** SNAILS OUT OF THEIR SHELLS IN FIVE MINUTES. "I HAVE BEEN SUCKING SNAILS SINCE I WAS A LITTLE BOY," PIERRE TOLD US, "AND EVEN NOW I HATE THE SIGHT OF THE SLIMY THINGS."

SLOOP

SOCKS
(CONTINUOUS WEAR)

ANDY SCHWARTZ , OF GLEN RIDGE, NEW JERSEY, CLAIMED THE RECORD IN 1975. IN A SWORN STATEMENT, ANDY'S WIFE DECLARED THAT HE HAD WORN THE SAME SOCKS EVERY DAY FOR **TWENTY YEARS AND 114 DAYS** . IN 1970, SHOE STORES THROUGHOUT NEW JERSEY BANNED ANDY FROM THEIR PREMISES. SINCE THEN HE HAS PURCHASED HIS SHOES THROUGH THE MAIL. ANDY PLANS TO REMOVE THE SOCKS AND TAKE A LOOK AT HIS FEET IN 1980.

SOILED HANDKERCHIEFS
(FROM THE STARS)

LES KNOT, OF LOS ANGELES, CLAIMED THE RECORD IN 1976. LES, 27, HAS BEEN COLLECTING SOILED HANDKERCHIEFS SINCE HE WAS A CHILD. "AT FIRST, I ONLY COLLECTED THEM FROM MY CLASSMATES," LES TOLD US. "THEN ONE DAY A FELLOW IN MY CLASS GAVE ME A DIRTY HANDKERCHIEF THAT HIS FATHER HAD USED. HIS FATHER WAS A STAR IN SILENT MOVIES. FROM THAT DAY ON, I COULD NEVER SETTLE FOR ANY OLD DIRTY HANDKERCHIEF. I'M SURE YOU CAN UNDERSTAND THAT."

SPITTING
〈CONTINUOUS〉

JESSE JAFFER OF SALVATION, NORTH CAROLINA, HOLDS THE RECORD. IN A CONTEST HELD ON JULY 10, 1975, AT DOWN WIND, PENNSYLVANIA, JESSE MANAGED TO SPIT **10,749** TIMES IN THREE HOURS. "I HOPED TO AVERAGE A SPIT-A-SECOND," JESSE TOLD US, "AND THOUGH I'M A LITTLE DISAPPOINTED, I'M PLEASED TO HAVE THE RECORD." (**NOTE:** JESSE WAS 18 WHEN HE SET THE RECORD, SO HE PROBABLY HAS MANY YEARS OF SPITTING AHEAD OF HIM.)

SPORTS (DEAD RAT THROWING)

DAN MANN, 19, HOLDS THE RECORD. IN A CONTEST HELD ON JULY 4, 1978, IN PASADENA'S ROSE BOWL, DAN HURLED A DEAD RAT (WEIGHING FOUR POUNDS DEADWEIGHT) A DISTANCE OF **312 FEET** FOR THE NEW WORLD'S RECORD. "I HAVE SOME ADVICE FOR YOUNG PEOPLE," DAN TOLD US. "START WITH MICE. A YOUNG ARM ISN'T READY FOR A DEAD RAT."

SPORTS
⟨FOOT IN MOUTH MARATHON⟩

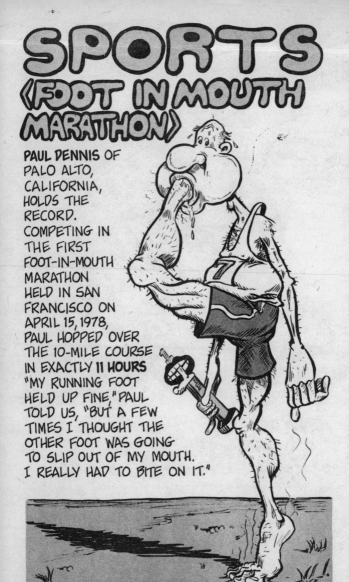

PAUL DENNIS OF PALO ALTO, CALIFORNIA, HOLDS THE RECORD. COMPETING IN THE FIRST FOOT-IN-MOUTH MARATHON HELD IN SAN FRANCISCO ON APRIL 15, 1978, PAUL HOPPED OVER THE 10-MILE COURSE IN EXACTLY 11 HOURS "MY RUNNING FOOT HELD UP FINE," PAUL TOLD US, "BUT A FEW TIMES I THOUGHT THE OTHER FOOT WAS GOING TO SLIP OUT OF MY MOUTH. I REALLY HAD TO BITE ON IT."

SPORTS
(JOGGING WITH DEAD PIGEON IN MOUTH)

ON SEPTEMBER 6, 1977, RON DUNCAN OF PHILA-
DELPHIA SET THE RECORD. RON JOGGED A
TOTAL OF **38** MILES WITH THE PIGEON CLENCHED
FIRMLY BETWEEN HIS TEETH. CROWDS LINED
THE ROUTE AND CHEERED RON EVERY STEP
OF THE WAY. "I FELT LIKE ROCKY," RON TOLD
US, "AND I KNEW THIS WAS GOING TO BE
MY DAY."

SPORTS
(MARATHON RUNNING WITH DEAD RAT IN MOUTH)

THIS ANNUAL RACE THROUGH THE STREETS OF CLEVELAND USUALLY HOSTS A LINEUP OF RUNNERS FROM ALL OVER THE WORLD. THE RECORD FOR THE 20-MILE COURSE WAS SET IN 1974 BY **MIKLOS KOMETH** OF HUNGARY, CARRYING A TWO-POUND RAT BETWEEN HIS TEETH, MIKLOS COVERED THE DISTANCE IN **ONE HOUR, 42 MINUTES.**

SPORTS
(MOSQUITO CATCHING)

IN THE SECOND ANNUAL CONTEST HELD AT LAKE FOREST, ILLINOIS, ON JULY 4, 1978, **SUSAN FLANDERS** MANAGED TO CATCH 1,482 MOSQUITOES WITH HER BARE HANDS. "I ACTUALLY CAUGHT 1,500," SUSAN CLAIMED, "BUT 18 OF THEM GOT CRUSHED."

SPORTS
(MOTORCYCLE CRASHING)

BEN DAVIDSON OF HARLEY, MONTANA, HOLDS THE RECORD. IN 14 YEARS (THROUGH 1977) OF MOTORCYCLE CRASHING, BEN HAS BROKEN EVERY BONE IN HIS BODY AND HAS RECEIVED OVER 1,000 STITCHES. "I WANTED TO HAVE 1,776 STITCHES BY THE BI-CENTENNIAL," BEN TOLD US, "BUT I DIDN'T MAKE IT." THAT'S ALL RIGHT, BEN, EVERYBODY KNOWS YOU TRIED!

SPORTS

(100 YARD DASH WITH LIVE GOLDFISH IN UNDERWEAR)

PAUL FLETCHER OF LITTLE POND, NEW MEXICO, HOLDS THE RECORD. IN A RACE HELD ON AUGUST 15, 1975, PAUL COVERED THE 100 YARDS IN **10.7 SECONDS**, TOPPING THE OLD RECORD 11.3 SECONDS. THE TOP SPEED OF THE DAY WAS ACTUALLY 10.3 SECONDS, BUT WHEN IT WAS DISCOVERED THAT THE GOLDFISH HAD EXPIRED, THE CONTESTANT WAS DISQUALIFIED.

SPORTS (ROLLING)

PEG PAULLY, OF BALTIMORE, HOLDS THE RECORD. IN 12 DAYS (NOVEMBER 1-13, 1974), PEG ROLLED FROM NEW YORK CITY TO CHICAGO, A DISTANCE OF OVER **700 MILES**. THIS BREAKS THE OLD RECORD OF 493 MILES SET BY MIKE MILTON IN 1971. MIKE WAS ON HAND WHEN PEG ARRIVED IN CHICAGO, AND HIS FRIENDS ROLLED HIM OUT TO GREET HER.

SPORTS (SNOW EATING)

IN 1976, BUFFALO, NEW YORK, HOSTED THIS INTER-
NATIONAL TEST OF SKILL. CONTESTANTS FROM
24 COUNTRIES LINED UP ON BUFFALO'S MAIN
STREET AND WAITED FOR THE SIGNAL TO BEGIN
GOBBLING UP THE SNOW THAT COVERED THE
THOROUGHFARE. IN THE END, JACQUES PORNIER
OF MONTREAL, CANADA, HAD EATEN HIS WAY
THROUGH 100 YARDS OF SNOW IN 33 MINUTES, "IT
WASN'T DIFFICULT," JACQUES TOLD US. "THE
COURSE WAS QUITE FLAKY."

SPORTS (SPITTING-STATIONARY TARGET)

IN A CONTEST HELD AT BARNEY'S KNOCK-EM DOWN AT ATLANTIC CITY, NEW JERSEY, **THERESA "TRENCH MOUTH" VINCENT** SPIT DOWN FOURTEEN CATS (STUFFED) AND WALKED AWAY WITH THE STATIONARY TARGET SPITTING TITLE FOR 1976. QUITE HUMBLE, THERESA TOLD US, "IT TOOK A LOT OF LUCK AND A LOT OF SPIT TO CAPTURE THIS RECORD."

SPORTS (TOE JAM FLICKING STATIONARY TARGET)

SCORING 5 BULL'S EYES OUT OF 8 FLICKS, **JOHN WINSLOW** OF LONDON WON THE WORLD'S TOE JAM FLICKING TITLE IN A CONTEST HELD IN CICERO, ILLINOIS, ON APRIL 10, 1976. CONTESTANTS FROM ALL OVER THE WORLD VIED FOR THE TITLE, BUT JOHN WAS AN EASY WINNER. "I DID IT FOR ENGLAND," JOHN TOLD US.

TITLE SHOT TARGET

FLICK

STITCHES
《COLLECTIONS》

FANNY LERNER, OF CATSGUT, ILLINOIS,
HOLDS THE RECORD AS OF AUGUST 11, 1974.
FANNY'S COLLECTION OF STITCHES WAS
"WHEN I WAS A LITTLE GIRL," FANNY EX-
PLAINED, "MY LEG HAD TO BE STITCHED.
LATER, THE DOCTOR REMOVED THE STITCHES
AND LET ME KEEP THEM. THAT GOT ME
STARTED. NOW LOTS OF PEOPLE SEND ME
THEIRS. THEY REALLY HELP KEEP ME IN
STITCHES."

STUFFED RATS
(COLLECTION)

HORACE ODDIE OF NEW YORK CITY HOLDS THE RECORD. HORACE HAS **2,746** STUFFED RATS IN HIS COLLECTION (1976). "I STUFFED THEM ALL BY MYSELF," HORACE TOLD US. "YOU SEE, BACK IN 1952 I TOOK A COURSE IN TAXIDERMY THROUGH THE MAIL AND I GUESSED THAT NO ONE ELSE WAS STUFFING RATS. I GUESS YOU MIGHT SAY THAT I BECAME ENGROSSED WITH STUFFING RATS." IT'S GROSS, HORACE, NOT ENGROSSED!

SWAMP SLIME (COLLECTION)

STUDENTS OF **MARSHVILLE HIGH SCHOOL**, BIG MARSH, FLORIDA, HOLD THE RECORD. DURING THEIR SUMMER VACATION IN 1975, THEY COLLECTED OVER **400 POUNDS** OF SWAMP SLIME. SINCE THEN, THE SLIME HAS BEEN ON DISPLAY ON THE SCHOOL'S AUDITORIUM STAGE. "WE'RE PROUD OF THE KIDS," DR. ANTHONY MARINO, THE SCHOOL'S PRINCIPAL, TOLD US. "THEY MADE GOOD USE OF THEIR SUMMER."

TAPEWORM
(LONGEST)

SALLY MAE WALLACE OF GREAT GRITS, MIS-
SISSIPPI, HOLDS THE RECORD. ON SEPTEMBER
5, 1973, DOCTORS EXTRACTED **37 FEET** (CONTIN-
UOUS) OF TAPEWORM FROM SALLY. "ABOUT AFTER
20 FEET OF THAT THING HAD COME OUT OF MY
MOUTH," SALLY TOLD US, "I JUST KNEW I HAD THE
RECORD. I WAS REALLY FILLED WITH JOY."

TARTAR ⟨COLLECTION⟩

ALTHOUGH NO RECORDS HAVE BEEN KEPT, THE PEOPLE OF FISH FRY, LOUISIANA, SEEM THE LIKELY RECORD HOLDERS. FOR OVER A CENTURY, THEY HAVE BEEN COLLECTING TARTAR SCRAPED FROM THEIR TEETH. THEY COMBINE THE TARTAR WITH SOME SECRET INGREDIENTS AND SELL IT AS **"FISH FRY'S ORIGINAL TARTAR SAUCE"** IT'S GREAT ON FISH, WE WERE TOLD.

TEETH (X RAYS)

SALLY CARIES OF ATLANTA, GEORGIA, HOLDS THE RECORD. THE WALLS OF SALLY'S APARTMENT ARE PAPERED WITH TEETH X-RAYS. THEY NUMBER WELL OVER **ONE MILLION** INDIVIDUAL PICTURES. "I'M PLEASED WITH THE RECORD," SALLY TOLD US, "BUT IT WASN'T ONE OF MY GOALS. I JUST WANTED THE APARTMENT TO LOOK PRETTY."

TOASTED FLY
(EATING)

TOM ALBERT, OF ITCHY PAWS, NEBRASKA, HOLDS THE RECORD. IN A CONTEST HELD ON MAY 30, 1978, TOM CONSUMED **2,500** TOASTED HOUSE FLIES IN LESS THAN FIVE MINUTES. HIS CLOSEST COMPETITOR DROPPED OUT, CLAIMING THAT SOMEONE HAD SLIPPED A HORSE FLY ON TO HIS PLATE. (**NOTE**: A LATER INSPECTION OF THE CONTENTS OF THE COMPETITOR'S STOMACH REVEALED NO HORSE FLY, AND THE JUDGES GAVE THE VICTORY AND THE RECORD TO TOM ALBERT.)

TOE JAM
(EATING)

SID BELLMORE OF MARMALADE DELLS, WIS-
CONSIN, HOLDS THIS DARING RECORD. ON
AUGUST 15, 1974, SID MANAGED TO GULP DOWN
THREE TEASPOONSFUL OF FRESH TOE JAM.
HIS CLOSEST COMPETITOR MANAGED TWO
TEASPOONSFUL, BUT THE SECOND WAS DIS-
ALLOWED BECAUSE THE CONTESTANT
COUGHED IT UP.

TOE JAM
(GROUP COLLECTION)

STUDENTS OF **GLORY WALK HIGH SCHOOL** IN GLORY WALK, PENNSYLVANIA, HOLD THE RECORD. IN 1976, THEY COLLECTED **14 GALLONS** OF TOE JAM. "I'M PLEASED," THE PRINCIPAL OF GLORY WALK HIGH TOLD US. "WE ENCOURAGE THE STUDENTS TO WORK TOGETHER, AND THIS RECORD CERTAINLY SHOWS THE VALUE OF TEAMWORK.

GLORY WALK HIGH LEADS IN JAM.!!

TOILET SEAT
(COLLECTION)

LOUIS CHARMIN, OF CHICAGO, ILLINOIS, HOLDS THE RECORD. THROUGH 1976, LOUIS' TOILET SEAT COLLECTION NUMBERED **1,153**. "I SUPPOSE MY PRIZE SEAT IS AN IVORY ONE THAT ONCE BELONGED TO ONE OF THE SHAHS OF IRAN," LOUIS TOLD US "BUT THEY'RE ALL INTERESTING, AND EACH ONE, I SUPPOSE, HAS A TALE TO TELL."

TONGUE
(HAIRIEST)

SELMA RUBY, OF DALLAS, TEXAS, HOLDS
THE RECORD. SELMA'S TONGUE IS FULLY
COVERED WITH HAIR (1976). "I'VE BEEN
THINKING ABOUT HAVING IT REMOVED
BY AN ELECTROLYSIST," SELMA TOLD US,
"THOUGH LATELY PEOPLE HAVE BEEN
TELLING ME THAT IT'S BEAUTIFUL."

TRAIN PULL (WITH NOSTRILS)

WITH A HOOK SECURED TO HIS NOSTRILS, JEFF "STRONG NOSE" SADLER PULLED A STEAM ENGINE 100 YARDS ALONG THE TRACKS AT HACKENSACK, NEW JERSEY, ON JUNE 12, 1971. THIS, TO OUR KNOWLEDGE, WAS THE ONLY SUCCESSFUL NOSTRIL PULL OF A TRAIN.

107

UNDERARM HAIR
(LENGTH)

FLORENCE FLOSS OF BAN, IDAHO, HOLDS THE RECORD. ON JULY 15, 1976, THE HAIR GROWING OUT OF FLORENCE'S LEFT ARMPIT STRETCHED TO A LENGTH OF **34 INCHES** THIS WAS MORE THAN ENOUGH FOR THE RECORD, BUT FLORENCE HOPES TO HAVE A YARD OF HAIR DANGLING FROM HER ARMPIT VERY SOON. "I SHAVE THE OTHER ARMPIT," FLORENCE REPORTED TO US.

VOMITING (IN SPACE)

YURI BARFNIKOV, A SOVIET COSMONAUT, HOLDS THE RECORD. WHILE WALKING ON THE MOON ON SEPTEMBER 13, 1977, YURI EXPERIENCED SOME STOMACH DISCOMFORT AND VOMITED. OFFICIALS FROM THE SOVIET UNION IMMEDIATELY CLAIMED THE RECORD, AND WHEN YURI RETURNED TO EARTH, HE WAS GIVEN A HERO'S WELCOME. (NOTE: IN A RARE GESTURE OF INTERNATIONAL COOPERATION, THE SOVIETS MADE THE TELEVISION FOOTAGE OF THIS AMAZING RECORD AVAILABLE FOR U.S. VIEWING.)

VOMITING
(TAPINGS)

AGNES ZENTER OF HILLSIDE, NEW JERSEY, HOLDS THE RECORD. THROUGH 1976, AGNES HAD CAPTURED ON TAPE 1,243 DIFFERENT PEOPLE IN THE ACT OF VOMITING. "I HATE VOMITING," AGNES TOLD US. "I ACTUALLY PREFER HEARING PEOPLE BLOW THEIR NOSES, BUT MY BROTHER BOB HAS TAPED SO MANY OF THEM THAT I HAD TO TRY FOR A DIFFERENT RECORD." (NOTE: FOR BOB'S RECORD, SEE BOOK I.)

WATER BUG
⟨EATING⟩

CAPTAIN B. A. CRUNCH, OF THE U.S. ARMY HOLDS THE RECORD. IN A CONTEST HELD ON APRIL 25, 1975, CAPTAIN CRUNCH ATE 4,321 WATER BUGS (COOKED IN A CORN POPPER) IN A FOUR-HOUR SITTING. "I COULD HAVE EATEN MORE," THE HAPPY OFFICER TOLD US, "BUT THE JUDGES REFUSED TO ALLOW THEM TO BE BUTTERED."

WISDOM TEETH (COLLECTION)

LINDA SAUNDERS, OF COLGATE, MISSOURI, HOLDS THE RECORD. THROUGH 1977, LINDA'S COLLECTION OF WISDOM TEETH NUMBERED 36,785. "IN A WAY MY MOTHER GOT ME STARTED," LINDA TOLD US. SHE SAVED ALL MY BABY TEETH, AND THAT INSPIRED ME." (NOTE: LINDA'S BABY TEETH ARE ON DISPLAY AT THE GROSSEST HALL OF RECORDS.)

EPILOGUE

Grossest Hall of Records

In 1976, plans were completed for the first permanent exhibit hall of gross memorabilia, and early in 1980 the hall will be opened to the public. Its site, the rear room of Lilly's Bar and Grill in downtown Swillington, Iowa, was selected from a list of thousands of applicants, and we believe it should attract millions of visitors annually.

At present, memorabilia collected for the permanent collection is being stored in a warehouse in Secaucus, New Jersey. The following description of items donated by record holders will probably send a chill up your spine. We certainly wish to extend our gratitude to the record holders, their families, and others for their generosity.

Memorabilia Donated

ADULT BODY (Baldest)—Adele Smith (Mrs. Ben Smith) donated a series of photos of Ben's bald body.

APPENDIX TRANSPLANT (From Hog)—Josef Podlawski provided the stuffed head of a hog that once owned his appendix.

ARMPIT (Sniffing)—Miriam Morton provided a complete list of all the people she has sniffed, including persons now deceased.

BELLY-BUTTON LINT (From The Stars)—Barry Barber donated a photo of his hand-vac.

BOOGER (Highest Priced)—Upshaw's, a New York City gallery, provided a wax impression of the highest-priced booger.

BOOGERS (From History)—Dr. Hans Friedlink donated a booger taken from the bullet-ridden body of John Dillinger.

BURPING (Group)—The mayor of Gassup, New Mexico, provided a cassette containing highlights from a burping recording.

CALLUS (Collection)—Florence Franklin donated a piece of callus autographed by Miklos Kometh, the rat-in-mouth marathon runner.

CAT TEETH (Collection)—Margie Norman donated fifty cat teeth taken from cats in each of fifty states.

CATERPILLAR-EATING (Live)—Walter Lucas provided a color photo of the green caterpillar that gave him the world's record.

CHICKEN BONES (Collection)—Ed "Rooster" Hayes, the mayor of Chapman, provided one ton of chicken bones taken from the community pot.

CIGAR BUTTS (Collection)—Larry Lincoln donated a three-page autobiography covering most of the major events in his life.

COBWEBS (Eating)—Robert Armstrong donated an autographed first edition of his book, *Cutting Calories with Cobwebs.*

DANDRUFF (Eating)—The citizens of Gotshair provided 1,000 bags of "Honey Dandruff," their national candy.

DEAD RATS (Collection)—Dan Blake donated 13 dead rats for "good luck for the Grossest."

DEAD INSECTS (Collection)—Paul Roach donated 32,000 dead ants sealed in plastic and set as an outline map of New Hampshire.

DIET (Healthiest)—The people of Nature's Best provided a photo of their youngest resident eating his mother's lice.

EAR-WAX LICKING (From Pay Telephones)—Dan Dannon donated the "Let Dan Lick" plaque awarded to him by the Liberal Party of New York to protest the actions of the telephone company.

EYE GOOK (Collection)—Sandman Phillips provided an ounce of eye gook taken from a Tibetan Yak.

FEET (Smell)—Wanda Lake donated a pair of her shoes sealed for release in the event burglars should attempt to enter the Hall after hours.

FISH HEAD (Collection)—Janice Karp donated fluke, bass, herring, whiting and sardine heads.

GARBAGE (From The Stars)—Jack Keno donated a "mixed bag" from his world-famous Gag Bag shop.

GARLIC (Eating)—Joseph Van Dyke promised a week of his service as a "security guard."

HAIRIEST LEGS (Adult)—Rita Sims donated a lock of hair taken from her left ankle.

HEIGHT AND WEIGHT DIVINATION (Through Seat Analysis)—Subodh Rey provided a 15-minute videotape of his television quiz show, "You Bet Your Nose."

KISS OF DOG (Longest)—Evelyn Hunt donated an autographed copy of her book, *I Never Kissed a Collie.*

LEFTOVERS (Eating)—Lillian Bingham provided a list of "New York City's Top Spots for Leftovers" with tips on how to get them while they're still hot.

LONGEST BATH (Group)—The people of Culligan donated a railroad tank car filled with bath water "we used to set our fabulous record."

MUSCLES (Thigh)—Judy Burns provided a plaster cast of her leg "to be signed by the thousands of people who visit the Hall."

NOSE-STUFFING (Limburger Cheese)—Hans Kleiber donated the 13 ounces of Limburger cheese extracted from his nose on May 1, 1974.

NOSTRIL HAIR (Collection)—Alice Driston donated "the first nostril hair I ever tweezed. I took it from my grandmother. She was seriously ill, and I guess I just wanted something to remember her. She's gone, but now she'll never be forgotten."

PERSPIRATION (Collection)—The Sweet Sweat Bottling Company provided one dozen miniature bottles containing samples from the collection.

PLATE-LICKING—Gloria Evans donated a plate given to her by Kitchen Workers, Local 15, Chicago. It bears the inscription: "For Gloria: You've Licked Our Best and We Salute You."

POSTAGE STAMPS (Diet)—Herbert Winstead provided a copy of his best-selling book, *Stamping Out Fat*.

RAT TAILS (Collection)—Glenda Gabor donated a rat-tail rug for "your lobby." The attractive rug has a large, white "G" in its center area.

ROACH (Largest)—Rita Carson provided a color photo of herself and her pet roach leading the Rose Bowl Parade (1976) through downtown Pasadena.

SINGING GROUP (Grossest Name)—Boogers on Toast donated a copy of their hit record, "It's Not Forever."

SOCKS (Continuous Wear)—Andy Schwartz donated a photo of his bare feet taken in 1955.

SPITTING (Continuous)—The citizens of Down Wind provided a 12-minute film entitled "Highlights of the Annual Spitathon."

SPORT (Dead-Rat Throwing)—Dan Mann donated "the dead rat I tossed for the world's record."

SWAMP SLIME (Collection)—Dr. Anthony Marino provided a photo of the entire student body of Marshville High School taken "to provide inspiration for future generations of students."

TAPEWORM (Longest)—Sally Mae Wallace donated a videotape of her tryout for an appearance on "I've Got a Secret."

TOE JAM (Eating)—Sid Bellmore donated a copy of his wife's book, *The Secret on My Lips.*

TRAIN PULL (With Nostrils)—Jeff Sadler donated his nose. It was torn from his face in 1977 when he attempted to pull the Staten Island Ferry into its dock.

VOMITING (In Space)—Yuri Barfnikov's soiled helmet was donated by the Soviet Committee for Joint Space Cooperation.

WATER BUG (Eating)—The U.S. Army donated a recruiting poster of Captain Crunch.